Stone Magic

By Candace L. Sherman

The A–Z Guide of
Healing Stone Properties

Stone Magic
2019©Copyright Candace L. Sherman

Publisher: Crystal Books

Contact the author at: cls@clsherman.com
Or visit: www.clsherman.com

Book design by theartoftheword.com

There are rocky roads in all our lives. At best we hope for the love of friends and family to carry us through. I am one of those blessed with friendship and family members who care about me as well as what I believe in.

I thank you all for your support in my latest endeavors. It has been a long and arduous haul for me to comprehend what my books were to hold within the covers and yet, when the time was correct, messages were given quite clearly.

Thanks to all my spirit guides who listen to my prayers and have patience with me.

My hope is that this book will assist in your efforts towards finding your true inner self, and true path in life.

Table Of Contents

12

In the Beginning.

Who knew that one-day a childhood fascination would develop into written books?

That I would admit openly I believe we all have psychic ability and that stones have their own energy? This is energy that humans can tap into and use on both conscious and subconscious levels while here on Earth in our quest to be all that we can be.

Or, that one day I would channel information on the metaphysical properties of stones?

Bedroom bookshelves as a child were

filled with stones found in my back yard or on the beach.

During difficult emotional times, I would use my collection of stones for comfort. Turning them over in my hand I was fascinated by the uniqueness of each rock.

Stones never bored me, and I felt they never tired of me either.

Today I understand why I was drawn to this seemingly innocent collection of rocks as I have been given definitions of their metaphysical properties or energies through deep meditation.

For example, many rocks found in your back yard or on the beach contain quartz. Even beach sand is mainly quartz. Quartz is the most plentiful stone on our planet and helps you to find clarity.

Why then are humans constantly confused? I believe it is because we need to work through issues in order for our soul to eventually move on into a higher plane. Everyone has an opinion as to why we humans are here, and if we have multiple lives. There is room for each train of thought. My personal belief is that there is life after life, that there are higher planes and/or powers beyond our present existence. The higher power may be one God, or many as in Angels, or even as in Greek Mythology.

If you also believe in continual life then your question may be, why?

Why might we come back over and over again?

Maybe life here on earth is a school.

If so, we are in session from the time of birth and graduate when we leave our bodies.

What life lessons will you carry over to make your soul better?

Maybe you have been very ill in this life.

Disease is broken down to dis–ease. All humans suffer dis–ease in one form or another. Find the cause. Perhaps the use of stone energy can help in your search. Maybe they will help restore mental or emotional balance to bring forth health!

Share my beliefs or not, you can still receive energy by wearing stones.

One of the most magical things about stones is they don't demand you pay homage to their power.

Wear stones and forget their individual properties and you will still receive their help energetically.

Say thank you to them or not at the end of the day, it makes no difference. You don't have to clean up after a stone, take it for a walk, or find an excuse for how you didn't call when you were going to be late for dinner.

Often times I tape loose stones to my

person. Place some masking tape over a stone and attach it to your body for a day. See if something comes through as mental clarity.

If the stone is rough, use some form of cloth or paper towel between you and the stone, then apply tape over the top of that, the energy will still come through. Pure natural fabric such as cotton or silk is best when you try this method. Pure material won't cloud the energy emanating from the stone.

If you are a person who meditates, try holding a stone while you do so as the energy connection during those meditations could surprise you.

Stones need to be cleansed occasionally whether you meditate with them, wear them, or have them sitting in a room, because they absorb energy. Refer to my web site for cleansing methods of stones, pearls, and beads: **clsherman.com**

I believe stones have missions while here on earth just as we humans do. All stones hold different energy that allow you to gain information from them.

Think of any form of fossil.

Information gets trapped inside the stone as the organism was formed into a mineral. This allows you to continue discovering new information from ancient remains.

Why couldn't it be the same for stones that have undergone earth shifts for thousands of years?

Let stones assist in your life lessons. Maybe your lesson is about holding onto something too tightly. We all get attached. Maybe it is time for you to move forward with the use of a new mineral.

When I misplace a stone, or piece of jewelry, I get upset and feel a loss.

Today, I work at being more philosophical about losing stones or jewelry. Generally, I feel they were taken away due to my attachment to that particular stone or jewelry item. So, now when this happens I ask the universe to return the item to me while I make a pact not to use the stone or jewelry for at least six weeks.

Normally this method works and the stone or jewelry is returned. I do then honor the pact.

Childhood obsession or not, you too can use stones to find answers in life. Look at the beauty of any stone and feel the energy trapped within.

Expand your consciousness to feel, something...

Don't ignore the need for medical assistance when using stone energy.

Stones can help you find the proper

professional help necessary by giving insight as to who you need to seek help from in order to heal. When I feel frustrated with my health, I sit with an emerald crystal and ask which way to turn?

With patience, I am usually guided to the next step. Trust your gut reaction to see if this new path is correct.

Years back, I began writing a coffee table book that combined healing properties of stones with pieces of jewelry I made. While writing *"Dreams Made of Stone"*, I felt there would be three books as a series. Any creative person will identify with my process—once you begin writing, painting, creating, you continue on and on.

Just prior to completing the first book I realized the second book would be stone definitions without any jewelry, and is what you are reading now, *"Stone Magic."*

Eventually, I realized all my books would

have stone energy as a core element. The first to go to print was an adventure book about children who get trapped within crystal caves. While there, they have to learn about healing stone energy.

"The Crystal Caves" is a fun read for all ages and got me started on a series. Watch for *"The Haunted Hotel"*.

Coming soon will be a novel loosely based on my travels while doing fine art and craft shows called, *"Stepping Stones"*.

In this particular book you're reading, *"Stone Magic"* lists stone properties of common, and not so common stones available today as cut gemstones or mineral specimens.

Use this book as a tool towards self-evolution, similar to meditation.

Take this book traveling with you to discover why you are drawn to individual gems or minerals at certain times.

Stones are listed alphabetically. Where there are two names to a stone, such as Rubilite Tourmaline, you will find the stone listed under "T" for Tourmaline.

Stone properties are kept short and to the point as this is how the information was channeled for easier memory.

Under the definition of each stone you will find a characteristic that states what family it belongs to as a core mineral, and if it is organic, precious, semi-precious, mineral or gemstone. Precious, semi-precious stones and pearls are more commonly used in the jewelry trade.

The gemstone/mineral category covers stones that are sometimes used in jewelry but are mainly considered to be mineral specimens and/or ornamental.

Many stone names end in "ite", as in Kunzite. In these instances, the stones are named either for the person who discovered them, or for the area in which they were first discovered. Henry Kunz is credited for discovering the mineral we know of today as Kunzite, page 69. Vesuvianite, page 107, is named for the area in which it was first found, Mount Vesuvius.

Information for stone properties contained within this book have been channeled. I write a stone name at the top of ten or so loose pages. Those pages get spread out over a table along with some blank ones. Closing my eyes, I sit quietly and begin to breathe deeply. I force any thoughts out of my head that act as distractions. Asking simply for answers of what these stone properties were, I began to write. Keeping my own thoughts as blank as possible, when information began to come through, I trusted it was channeled.

I feel channeled information comes by way of spirit guides. My guides connect with me through my subconscious thoughts.

Stone information has never come in alphabetic order.

Often, more definitions came through than what I planned for.

Always craving confirmation as I worked on a piece of jewelry made with a stone I had channeled I would write down what I felt, or saw inside my head. Cross-referencing that information with what I had channeled, I would then watch what finished jewelry a client was drawn to and ask them to read the healing properties of that stone or stones.

Their response was always one of wide eyes as they asked, "Is this *magic?*"

Connections were made between written definitions, the emotional state of the client, and the stones they were drawn to. Over and over again, this proved to me the channeled information I received was correct.

Feeling I had total confirmation on healing properties, this person and client cross-referencing took years.

If for some reason the stone you love is not included in this book, don't feel slighted. I was informed to list these stones by my spirit guides.

Information on whether a stone has been treated in some way to be the color it is, is not included in this book. Many stones are beautiful the way they come out of the earth. Still other stones are treated in order to enhance their color.

Heat treatment of stones to enrich color has been done for centuries. Ancient Greeks placed stones on their roofs to let the sun do its magic. Lapis is one stone usually dyed today to beautify its rich navy blue tone. When a color enhancement has been done properly, I feel the color is permanent.

When I began my own metaphysical quest I was in my twenties. Books were not available at that time on stone properties although books eventually did come out. By then I had already developed my own beliefs about certain stones holding specific energies. Books available today on stone properties have merit. Try different books to see which one(s) you resonate with. I follow the properties I have channeled.

Stones are wonderul and are so magical that I dream about them at night.

Memorization is not my strong suit, so I look up the stone properties once awake and then put these stones on my person for energy assistance during that day.

Can you naturally be drawn to the stones you need to heal?

Do you pay attention?

Experiment with stones. Find magic yourself with the use of stones and their properties listed within these pages!

The A–Z Guide to Healing Stone Properties

Use this A-Z stone guide to locate stones you have seen, find intriguing, or already have.

Discover why you feel connected to them, and how they may help you heal.

Stones are listed in alphabetic order.

When two or more words are in a stone title, locate it listed under the first letter of the second word, i.e. *Icelandic Spar* is found under "S".

Also, find the family group a stone belongs to such as quartz, and if the stone is precious, semi-precious, mineral, gemstone, or organic.

When stones are considered durable enough, and attractive enough to use in jewelry, they are divided into the categories of precious, semi-precious, and gemstone.

Read mineral or organic as a description and know you can use these stones in jewelry, however, they will have limits as to durability.

Minerals and organics are normally in a hardness category of less than 4 on the Mohs scale of 1-10. Trust that any other definition is harder than a 4.

Abalone

Kidney tension is eased while calcium absorption is strengthened. Intense colors found in this shell connect with the cornea so you may see more clearly what is important to your life path. Being part of the shell family, the suggestion is to take care of *your* physical shell along with all that is contained within.

Abalone is part of the shell or organic family.

Agate

Overall, agates work on grounding. Feel calm and centered, that is grounding energy. Many color varieties are available. Generally, when talking about agates, one is referring to the gray or brown tone varieties.

Blue Lace Agate - Is a shield of protection. It also provides a steady stream of clarity for the wearer. (Pale blue with white veins. Remove the white lace formation in this stone and you have blue chalcedony. *Page 46)*

Botswana Agate - Happy, healing and teaching are proper descriptive words here. See life in its many splendors while taking one moment at a time. A grounding stone that teaches you how life moves on, and so must you. View problems as a moment in time. And then with the blink of an eye you too can move on. (Gray, brown, and black) This stone was discovered in Botswana.

Orange /Brown Agates - Work with layers of self and the earth. Feel grounded and centered when looking at your core being. View layers of significant moments from your beginning through the present. Unwrap, experience, and find a way to embrace every part of yourself. This enables the future to be what *you* will it to be.

Crazy Lace Agate - Grounding, with pockets of space to let your mind rest. (Tan, white and orange tones in swirl patterns)

Fire Agate - When cut and polished it reveals multiple colors, rainbows, and puffy clouds in a three-dimensional quality. Each day choices are made. Make your decisions three-dimensional.

Moss Agate - Cools the temper by bringing in a connection with the earth and shade. May life wrap nature about you as if literally in moss to feel grounded. (Deep green moss is actually trapped in clear quartz)

Plume Agate - The feathery core gives you inner comfort when necessary. Need to pamper or recharge your batteries? Use this stone. (Milky clear with white puffy spots)

Gray / White Agates - As if in a dream, your mind can have a run at a maze. Do you know your true path? The directions or choices you make in life are prepackaged, that does not mean you should not unwrap and choose how to live. (It's a light gray color that's slightly transparent. This particular tone of agate can be dyed, and as such the color is permanent)

Agates are part of the quartz family and are semi-precious.

Alexandrite

The colors of Christmas are widely accepted to be red and green. These two colors alternate within this stone bringing forth recharged energy, something you normally feel at that time of year. Be electric. Soon others will be attracted to your energy and life will seem to be a gift.

Alexandrite is part of the chrysoberyl family and is semi-precious.

Amazonite

Learn what gossip is and how it can stunt personal growth. Be the kind person you know is inside with the help of this stone.

Amazonite is part of the feldspar family and is semi-precious.

Amber

Helps remove physical pain from connecting bones in the body such as an elbow, knee, shoulder, etcetera. It cushions pain in a similar way to the fluid found between your vertebrae. Amber can give a mild electrical charge to the wearer, especially within creativity. Cause a change in your own creative energy with amber. Amber also connects with the stomach and digestive areas of the body.

(Colors available are brown, green, orange, red, and yellow tones) Color does affect the energy slightly, but not significantly enough to create separate categories. Simply think of yellow as being more in tune with the gut reaction area of the body found at the bottom of the ribs. Green connects with the heart area of the body. Orange and brown tones deal with the creative area, or stomach region. Red deals with the heart and base of the spine. Overall, amber helps remove joint pain.

Amber is literally a sap that has fossilized and is therefore part of the organic family.

Amethyst

Connects the crown chakra, or energy center found at the top of the head, with intuitive protective forces. It protects you against over indulgences while showing you **how** to be insightful.

Amethyst is part of the quartz family and is semi-precious.

Ametrine

Is a protective stone when testing new creative waters. Ametrine is a great stone to wear if in process of changing a career.

Ametrine is a combination of Amethyst and Citrine, is part of the quartz family, and is semi-precious.

Andalusite

Crossroad stone. In its crystal structure this mineral bears a cross. Make your crossroads in life multi-dimensional.

Andalusite is named after a Spanish province, Andalusia, and is a mineral/gemstone.

Angelite

Has a soft, embracing energy. This stone helps you to be kind to yourself as well as others. What you give out is usually what you crave back energetically. Look into the mirror and give what you need to yourself… Love!

Angelite is a mineral/gemstone.

Apatite

Consciousness awareness.

Blue /Green Apatite - Calms the overactive brain and gives it a chance to flow more evenly. If you wish to expand your personal universe but your mind *doesn't* stop, this stone will assist you. Get rid of the clutter. Open the doors to now gain a higher stream of consciousness.

Yellow /Green Apatite - Hold tight with all your might to the possibilities of universal understanding. Open your mind and heart to see life in a new way. Dream of what can be, and incorporate that with what is already alive in your present existence. Expand your consciousness.

Apatite is a mineral/gemstone.

Aquamarine

Helps share your minds' eye. How your brain forms a thought is important to share for inner growth. Think of Einstein, if he did not believe in sharing knowledge ... wow! Communication of what is vital and real to you is assisted with this stone. Aqua is especially useful for prenuptial people. What does partnership mean to you?

Aquamarine is also known as Blue Beryl (page 41) is part of the beryl family and is semi-precious.

Aragonite

Works on both the heart and lung areas of the body. When first worn there is a blast of energy to this area clearing away emotional blockage. Use this stone to begin the search inward as both the body *and* mind need permission to change.

Aragonite is a mineral/gemstone.

Aventurine

Its mica base balances the schizophrenic mind. This kind of balancing helps connect the dots emotionally, so to speak.

Aventurine is a quartz and is semi-precious.

Azurite

Aids those with a weepy heart. Restore emotions. listen to your heart's desire, feel safe to be you.

Azurite is a mineral/gemstone.

Barite

Is heavy. Use this stone if you are so flighty you forget who you are and what you are doing. Ground yourself with the help of this stone.

Barite is a mineral.

Benitoite

Think of an octopus and its ability to hold one or more objects with great might. Find what you need to hold onto for emotional strength, and then let the rest fall away into a pool of nothingness.

Benitoite is a mineral.

Beryl

Works on casings. (Your skin is a casing for bones, organs, blood, etc.)

Bixbite - Encircles the heart chakra or heart region of the body with love of the universe. You are part of the universe and always get back what you give out. *That* is karma. (Reddish color)

Blue Beryl - (Also called Aquamarine. Page 38)

Clear Beryl - Do inner homework to comprehend all is not doom and gloom. Take responsibility. Recognize your part in getting where you are right now. Do this, and you can take any number of steps toward change this minute! (Also called Goshenite)

Green Beryl - The auric field, or area of space found immediately around your body, receives the healing with green beryl. It surrounds you with a lovely transparent green light.
Emerald is also a green beryl. Here the discussion is more of a pale tone of green. Emerald is discussed on its own page 56.

Heliodor - Use the martini shaker called life to connect with the inner self and the world around you. Great stone for when you feel out of the loop. (This is a yellow to yellow-green color)

Pink Beryl - (Also called Morganite, page 75)

Golden or Yellow Beryl - Wisdom in sharing. How you shape your world and invite others in will be affected with this stone. (This is a lemon-yellow color)

Beryl is part of the beryl family. All but one are semi-precious. Emerald is precious.

Bloodstone

Works on the eye capillaries bringing in healing and grounding energy. It helps you see inwardly what is true and vital. Know if you are in the right place at the right time. You can then act with wisdom and clarity. (Is a darker green opaque stone with red dots running through it)

Bloodstone is also called Heliotrope, is part of the quartz family, and is semi-precious.

Ivory and Bone

Absorb shock to the system both physically and emotionally. When you feel bombarded by life and its struggles, ivory or bone are especially useful. Today, elephant tusk ivory is a banned substance due to cruelty in death to the animal. If you have antique ivory and feel the energy is clear; then perhaps that animal died of natural causes. Fossil walrus tusk is found as *stones* are, in a dig, so there is no cruelty involved.

Bone and Ivory are part of the organic family.

Calcite

Contains gentle energy. Very constructive for those apprehensive or weary of trying new things.

Green Calcite - Your inner self finds a refreshing coolness with this stone. Think of a very small, gently flowing stream. This is the energy you can bring forth to your inner existence.

Pink Calcite - You can be inside and outside your emotional body seemingly at the same time. Learn to be objective about what is useful guidance and what has outlived its emotional usefulness.

Yellow Calcite - Connects the synapses of the brain to the third eye allowing one to see clearly intuitive hits received all the time.

Calcite is a mineral/gemstone.

Cameo

Cut away what you no longer need or desire with

the use of this shell substance. Show the face you believe is truly you to the world. Live from the outside in and realize the world can be friendly if you are friendly to yourself first. Take care of your mind, body, and soul, as this will provide a sound base for you to stand on your own.

True cameo is carved from conch shell. Today, some cameos are cut from agates. Shell cameos are part of the organic family.

Carnelian

Grounds the root chakra, or energy found at the base of the spine. Think of coming home in the winter and eating root vegetables. How safe and full you feel! This stone balances and calms your core energy. Especially useful for anorexic/bulimic people assisting in finding a way for anger to be expressed in positive ways.

Carnelian is part of the quartz family and is semi-precious. The more-brown tone of carnelian can be referred to as Sard.

Celestite

Your celestial package is heightened. We all come

to this plane with spirit guides, a higher-self, and angel connections. Choose how to pay attention to celestial messages with the help of this mineral.

Celestite/ or Celestine, gets its name from Latin, alluding to its typical sky-blue color, and is a mineral.

Chalcedony

Acts as armor.

Blue Chalcedony - Performs as a shield of protection for the wearer. It gives the armor of confidence when something foreign comes at you. Feel safe, and then speak out for or against what has come your way.

Gray Chalcedony - Acts as a more relaxed concept of wearing armor. See what is coming your way and smile inwardly at how unimportant it all is. When you've really grown, and learned about a troubling issue, this stone will assist in the reminder phase. Look at how you used to respond, and no longer have the need to go there or even take that same route.

Chalcedony is part of the quartz family and is semi-precious. (Dyed chalcedony is often used as Onyx page 76)

Chalcopyrite

Allows you to see the rainbows already present in your life and how you brought them in. Now see how to release the negative thoughts blocking your path to total success while sending those thoughts out into oblivion!

Chalcopyrite is also known as Peacock Rock, is part of the pyrite family, and is a mineral.

Chrysoberyl

Gives inner knowledge of how your heart works emotionally. Expand, unclog, move toward openness and embrace yourself. Do this and expand outside yourself to draw in like-minded, or similar beings.

Chrysoberyl is related to Alexandrite and is semi-precious.

Chrysocolla

See what is important to you first and then how to express that outwardly.

Chrysocolla is a mineral/gemstone.

Chrysoprase

Provides a clear stream of consciousness between the mind and the heart. Desire for change begins in the mind. Deny this for a long time and your heart emotionally turns off. Become clear in the mind and your heart begins to open. You can then follow your true path. This is when passion for a new path carries you forward with great zeal.

Chrysoprase is part of the quartz family and is semi-precious.

Citrine

Creative juices flow with this stone. Have either a type of gut reaction to something or actually experience the need to be creative. Being a member of the quartz family, it also works with the fluids of the body; specifically, the creative juices.

Lemon Citrine - Works with memory in a creative way. When serious about changing your life, this stone helps to handle yourself along with your issues in a different way with self-assurance. (Yellow-green color)

Some people refer to this stone as lemon quartz. It was introduced to me as lemon citrine; I have called it this ever since.

Orange Citrine - Connects with the creative area of the body found around the ovaries and stomach. Whether involved in the arts or not, this color citrine gives you a creative boost.

Yellow Citrine - Works specifically with the gut reaction area of the body located at the bottom of the rib cage or solar plexus. Trust the first thought that comes into your head; that's a gut reaction or instinct. (Yellow to orange color)

Citrine is part of the quartz family and is semi-precious.

Coral

Deals with the skeletal structure, recreating alignment and balance. This substance helps absorb shock, be it emotional or physical.

Black Coral - Brings negative energy more into balance. Feel the world has handed out one bump too many? Wear this to realign yourself.

Oxblood Coral - From the base of the spine or kundalini, blood flow in the skeletal structure is balanced. Feel there is no emotional support? Turn here for guidance towards the proper support while opening up from your root energy to experience a new, positive outlook. (Deep red color)

Pink Coral - Love yourself creatively. Relax, breathe, and find a place that brings inner peace today. Let the world stand down for the moment to find that inner balance.

Salmon Coral - Creatively balances the skeletal structure. When you know why you are out of balance, understanding allows you to now make adjustments. Move out of the quandary. (Mix of orange to pink tone)

White Coral - When a bit shaken by society, use this substance. Find what brings personal comfort and set forth to manifest it in your life. This mineral is found closer to the ocean surface than other colors. Emotions are close to the surface. Only you can provide a safe haven for them.

Coral is part of the organic family.

Cuprite

Nighttime can be stressful if you're one who feels they didn't do enough all day. This stone helps you let go of that stress, to come into the night with a new emotional balance.

Cuprite is a mineral.

Danburite

Sit tight. Sometimes what you crave is trying to come your way. Are you in such a hurry it can't come in? Patience is not only a virtue it is a fruit bearing branch.

Danburite was discovered in Danbury, Connecticut, and is semi-precious.

Diamond

Intensifier! Worn alone, this carbon base mineral will heighten your mood, be it a good or bad one. When representing a love commitment as in an engagement ring or wedding band, diamonds work to heighten that love or provide a clarity in the relationship. (Keep in mind you should cleanse diamonds on a regular basis to prevent negative energy from building up. Look up information for cleansing at www.clsherman.com)

When diamonds are used as smaller side stones next to a larger colored stone, the diamonds act as an intensifier to the colored stone's energy. Take a blue sapphire with diamonds on the side; the diamonds intensify the psychic or intuitive energy of the sapphire. There are many different colors found in diamonds both natural and man altered. To date, they all work the same, as intensifiers.

Diamonds are precious.

Herkimer Diamonds

Bring a strong electrical charge to brain activity. Allow the conscious brain to go in one direction while the subconscious goes in the other. Digest what you learn and make new life choices. These stones are normally very clear and double-terminated, or pointed on both ends. With its carbon deposits, you feel the lightning bolt of electricity. This is not a stone for the faint of will and is best used sparingly.

Herkimer Diamonds were discovered in Herkimer, NY, are part of the quartz family, and are gemstones.

Diopside

Imagine yourself in clean fresh mountain air standing barefoot in green grass. Without normal tension of the day you can create a core of calm and formulate new decisions. Struggle is part of the process. Do not separate your existence from the struggle. This is how you can and do bring about change in the thought process. If you take responsibility for creating the struggle, you can choose to create calm in its wake today.

Diopside is semi-precious.

Dioptase

Think of a carbonated drink, see the effervescence bubble forth. Tap into your own joie de vivre with the use of dioptase.

Dioptase is a mineral.

Dolomite

Help your own natural bodily minerals to assimilate properly with the use of this stone. With proper mineral use, your body helps you function and live.

Dolomite is a mineral.

Druzy

Any form brings illumination.

Druzy Chrysocolla - Breathe, relax, and see other's verbalizations as input and not gospel.

Druzy Psilomelane - See the road blocks you create clearly. With this illumination, you can find a new road or new way of driving through life.

Druzy Quartz - Provides sparks of insight to see your life path more clearly.

When a thin layer of tiny, fairly uniform crystals occurs naturally on any stone, it is called druzy.

Druzy can also be a layer of tiny quartz crystals on and/or incorporated into another mineral. When that occurs, the base stone is the second word in the name.

Since druzy can be almost any stone, I will simply call it semi-precious. Is accepted as either druzy or drusy.

Eilat

Turbulence is recognized, identified, and released. Caution as to how you release energy is necessary. Eilat contains three great insight minerals that help to see your way through such release periods.

Eilat is a combination of Chrysocolla, Malachite, and Turquoise, and is semi-precious.

Emerald

True healer! This stone brings in a connection of the heart and gut reaction. Knowing what and how to do for yourself is always the first step towards total health. Heal the heart, then the body and soul will follow.

Emerald is part of the beryl family and is precious.

Epidote

Think of life as if you were going on a fishing expedition. When you find where you need to be to catch the fish you want, you can become the person you know in your heart you are.

Epidote is a mineral.

Hawk's Eye

With clear vision from very far away your higher self points the direction your true path must lead.

Hawk's Eye is also called Blue Tiger's Eye, is part of the quartz family and is semi-precious.

Tiger's Eye

Helps provide mental clarity by eliminating conceptual cobwebs. Narrow the viewing field and know the direction you need to take from a sound, firm base. Move your life forward with new knowledge as your guide.

Tiger's Eye is part of the quartz family and is semi-precious.

Fluorite

Is like the *deep* ocean where slight motion is all that is necessary to keep life in balance. Internal fluids find a peaceful stability and then provide a strength for your inner character to be released. Once centered, you live in a equalized way and allow others to comprehend your mind set.

Fluorite is semi-precious.

Fossils

All kinds of fossils bring forth ancient wisdom. Receive knowledge that has been trapped within whatever died suddenly through earth shifts.

Fossils are part of the organic family.

Garnet

The great equalizer. There are many colors and names for garnet. Here they are grouped under color mostly except for both Rhodolite and Uvarovite that have separate headings. That's how the information was given.

Brown Garnet - Acts as a generator. When stuck in one emotional place for too long, use this stone to create energy and the impetus to move out into something new. Stagnant energy isn't good on any plane be it physical, psychological, or spiritual. (Can have a touch of orange and is also called Hessonite)

Green Garnet - Works on the thyroid, heart and sexual organs. Create a balance of the emotional and the spiritual self. This stone helps you serve others while remaining mindful of your own self. (Light green is called Grossular, emerald green is called Demantoid)

Orange Garnet - Expansion. When you are really done with inner work and are ready to let the world see the true you, wear this stone to breathe from both inside and outside your body. (Can have a touch of red and is also called Spessartite Garnet)

Purple Garnet - This color deals with the circulation of blood flow from the heart to the fingertips. Being able to reach out for both what you want and need *is* circulation. (Also called Grape Garnet)

Red Garnet - Works to align the lumbar vertebrae and allow blood to flow evenly while building and assimilating iron in the system. This is especially useful for women during menses if prone to lower back pain from swelling. (Also called Pyrope)

Rhodolite Garnet - Assists in loving the world you live in. Go inward, make peace internally, change what no longer suits you, gather strength and *then* go outward. (Is a pink tone garnet)

Uvarovite - Provides illumination for the healing process. There is a connection between the mind and body. Learn why the illness came about in the mind, heal this and the body will follow. (Is a green garnet mineral of tiny clustered crystals)

Yellow Garnet - Deals specifically with the ovaries. Discover why you won't give yourself permission to be creative in your daily existence. Break the chains that bind, begin to *create* your life anew.

Garnet is semi-precious.

Granite

Many color varieties are available with as many slight variations on influence, however, the main feature is "slick". You won't get too hot or too cold emotionally when using this stone. Don't allow yourself to remain detached for long or you'll lose out on life.

Granite has many slight variations of mineral make-ups that shift the colors, and it is a mineral.

Gypsum

Gypsum and talc have much in common, they both soothe the soul.

Gypsum is a mineral.

Hematite

Cleanses impurities in the bloodstream. It also provides protection from others' negative thoughts and vibrations. It is a coal base mineral that provides fuel for the wearer. Get the job done while choosing whose issues to invite in.

Hematite is semi-precious.

Hemimorphite

Contains some of the same qualities as in its name. "Morph" yourself with the assistance of this mineral. Shift the way you look at your inner world, or actually bring in personal change with hemimorphite.

Hemimorphite is a mineral.

Hiddenite

What is hidden just below the surface emotionally is brought forth enabling the transformation you have been craving to emerge.

Hiddenite is part of the spodumene family and is semi-precious.

Horn

Helps you come from a place of inner strength. Decide when, where, how, and what encounters are true and worthy. Know your battles, and the rest of life's daily annoyances fall away as dust of unimportance.

Horn is part of the organic family.

Howlite

Have an internal chalkboard with this chalk-like mineral. Write out ideas, goals, issues, and then erase what doesn't work in your mind, or does not seem to connect. Once the board is clear, write out new ideas, to begin again.

Howlite is a mineral/gemstone.

Iolite

This is the twilight stone. Think of the calm that comes at the end of the day when you know you have accomplished as much as you could. Shed obstacles along with the day's stresses and expectations. Let the evening breeze flow over you with the wisdom that you did what was possible. Reconnect now with what you know to be important: peace of mind and spirit. When you are ready to go within and emanate outward, you connect with the same energy we find at day's end.

Iolite is also called Water Sapphire, and is semi-precious.

Tiger Iron

Deals with bodily iron and energy levels. Think of words from the song Kenny Rogers made famous, "Know when to hold them, and when to fold them". In the song, these words referred to card games. Use these words internally to decide if your physical, emotional and mental energy is correct to move forward today. Use Tiger Iron if you are an impatient or impulsive mover and shaker to work *with* your energy level and not against it.

Tiger Iron is part of the Tiger's Eye and iron ore family and is semi-precious.

Jade

Heals the damaged etheric body on into the psyche. The etheric body is the air or energy field directly around your physical body, also known as your aura.

Brown Jade - Soothes the stomach for those who hold tension in this area by relaxing related muscles. Absorb life better and "digest it". Don't let life rule or overwhelm you.

Green Jade - Natural protective shield along with hope for a good life.

Lavender Jade - Soft, soothing pillow of comfort and protection from the harsh environment. This stone is most useful for those around smog and smoke types of contamination.

Red Jade - Guide a sedentary life slowly, carefully back into the living from a safe emotional place. (It's a brownish-red color)

White Jade - White stones often make use of angelic forces as is the case here. Angels are known to be helpful and this angel power comes from inside your head. Give the mind space to breathe and function normally instead of from a place of "have-to-dos".

Yellow Jade - See into your own soul. Find what has been there all along. Direction of a true path and the will to pursue such is provided here.

Jade is semi-precious.

Jasper

Is grounding.

Bruno Jasper - With calm surety you can wind your way through life. (Beige tones in wave and swirl patterns)

Dalmatian Jasper - Used with bone or ivory gives the ability to reject outside influences. Choose your own path. (Off white with black spots)

Leopard Skin Jasper - Heals stomach aches by grounding anxiety. (Off-white with brown tones in close patterns)

Poppy Jasper - Be creative in thought. Expansion of the spirit will follow. (Red tones with some beige)

Red Jasper - Grounds the sad soul. See a pathway to freedom. Great stone for people with severe depression. (Red-to-brown even color)

Scenic Jasper - Create new vistas. Open your eyes. (Brown tones in patterns that appear to be painted on the stone)

Jasper is part of the quartz family and is semi-precious.

Jet

Has a coal base that can ignite your soul into action. Great when you've been sitting on ideas leery of taking action.

Jet is part of the organic family, and is a mineral.

Kunzite

Has a lithium base that helps to calm you from known and unknown anxieties. After serious emotional or physical loss, this stone gives a calm inner center to relax. With inner calm, choice for the next step is made easier. Kunzite helps ease shoulder trauma, and shoulders are where burdens are carried.

Kunzite is part of the spodumene family and is semi-precious.

Kyanite

Peel away layers of doubt and fear. Envision a life of dreams fulfilled. God will provide. **You** must be the one to do the homework. Look at any fear as if under a microscope. Face it. Figure out how you gave life to this, now, discover how to develop the cure. To date, kyanite comes in blue and green colors. Both work to peel away...

Kyanite is a gemstone, and is semi-precious.

Labradorite

Is like fish scales that are iridescent yet not quite transparent. You can grab the rainbows in life and allow these moments to be magical. This will carry you through the difficult places in your mind.

Labradorite is part of the feldspar family and is semi-precious.

Lapis

The family issues stone. Connect with your intuition. Decipher what is important *and* what is age-old button pushing. No one knows how to push your buttons better than family! These old buttons are now out dated and unimportant. MOVE ON!

Lapis is also called Lapis Lazuli, or Lazurite, and is semi-precious.

Larimar

Shows you how not to be a fool rushing in. Bearing

colors of the ocean this stone has recently come into focus. Keep your own focus centered to know when it's correct to move ahead with a long-range plan or idea.

Larimar is a type of Pectolite, and is semi-precious.

Azurite-Malachite

Aligns the heart with the lungs creating the perfect rhythmic breath. Especially useful for people with asthma and chronic lung issues.

Azurite–Malachite is semi-precious.

Malachite

Heals the body by flushing toxins through the kidneys, ovaries, and liver. There is a copper base to this mineral that assists the body in this endeavor. Malachite is also very useful in protecting against negative ions for those who do a lot of work on computers.

Malachite is semi-precious.

Moldavite

Celestial connection. It is a meteorite like Tektite and, connects much the same as Celestite.

Part of the meteorite and tektite family.

Moonstone

Always ties into lunar and the feminine energy that is a part of us all. Lunar energy is feminine. Being part of the feldspar group, the thought given by one of my spirit guides is, "With spar you can go far".

Adularia Moonstone - Connects with Lemuria and the energies thought lost long ago. Link with the heritage of an advanced culture through lunar energy to gain strength, peace of mind, and knowledge. (Clear white, transparent tone with blue as the light plays on it)

Green Moonstone - Heals past-life trauma one step at a time as in the twelve lunar cycles. Think of all the twelve-step programs available today. This twelve-step program can set you free from past-life baggage. (Transparent greenish tone)

Licorice Moonstone - Though this is the darkest color of the moonstone group, it works to bring a beacon of light into dark corners of the mind as well as in the dream phase. It's as if the moon swings the mind open to shine a light inside. (Can be a light to dark gray tone that some call gray moonstone)

Orange Moonstone - Allows a cooling energy to flow through the physical body with waves of calm. The moon is a cool energy as opposed to the heat of the sun. (Transparent-ish orange tone, some call it pink)

Rainbow Moonstone - Connects rainbows of possibility if you work with your dreams, lunar cycles, and the earth's magnetic pull. (Also called Peristerite, is a bit transparent white overall with strong rainbows of color running through it) Many refer to Rainbow Moonstone as part of the Labradorite or Spectrolite family... *all* are feldspars. What distinguishes these three stones is, the rainbow effects found within. Adularia Moonstone also has a rainbow affect, however, it's not as prominent as these other three stones.

White Moonstone - Balance feminine energy within your personal lunar cycle and the psychic connection inherent in all will come forth. (Either a transparent white tone or a bit murky white)

Moonstone is part of the feldspar family and is semi-precious.

Morganite

This stone carries the message, "Don't fight the change that is coming your way." Allow yourself freedom to embrace new personal developments while assimilating vitamin C, which strengthens gum tissue. When you can chew on life properly good digestion on all levels will be brought your way.

Morganite is part of the beryl family and is semi-precious.

Snowflake Obsidian

Brings forth magic of the white Christ light also known as a pure space, or energy of acceptance. Grasp the soothing energy found within a sense of calm and peace. Nitrogen is a necessary element for all plant life and is brought forth to humans with this stone allowing for expansion of the mind. Do not harbor pre-conceived ideas or notions; rather, open the doors and let fresh air in.

Snowflake Obsidian is semi-precious.

Onyx

Is for protection.

Black Onyx - Is the mirror of the soul. It allows you to hold private what you will while stopping others from coming forcefully in. You keep what is yours and they keep what is theirs.

Blue Onyx - When you have faced your fears, (I mean *really* faced your fears) and are ready to face the world as the **true you**, wear this stone. Receive protection from negative thoughts when shifting into a positive frame of mind.

Green Onyx - Creates an even temperament by balancing the highs and lows from sugar imbalances. How you digest food correlates with what your mood is.

Orange Onyx - Protect your thoughts, your family, or even your car by picturing it protected and thus making it so. Be creative in how you envision and use psychic fortification.

Sardonyx - Is the combination of white and black, or white, black, and orange onyx together in the same stone, sometimes called banded agate. Refer to each color in your piece to get an overview.

White Onyx - Is not in the angel phase as is the case with most white stones. This white stone connects with brain-power. Protect what you think about because thoughts can and do create motion in life. "Think and make it so", is the proper quote to keep in mind.

Yellow Onyx - Is for steering protection to specific organs within the body. Concentrate on an organ in need, and think of it recreating itself. Do this and that organ begins to be protected from negative elements, because now you are working to eliminate what is bad for that organ.

Onyx is part of the quartz family and is semi-precious. There is genuine onyx as well as dyed chalcedony. Most onyx used in jewelry today is dyed chalcedony (Or gray agate).

Opal

Enlightens and clears mental cobwebs. Some cobwebs can be very useful to bring in food necessary for survival while others need to be eliminated. Opal also helps with your bodily fluids. There is a better stream of thought when you balance the water in your system along with your higher consciousness. Be fluid and go with the flow. Do not be passive. Know when to be active and when to wait.

There are many different colors of opals. Some opals look very different than you might normally expect. This includes a solid baby blue stone and one with spots of different colors clustered into a fairly clear jelly-like space. To date, I have found they all clear mental cobwebs and work on body fluids.

Opal is part of the quartz family and is semi-precious.

Orthoclase

Bring grounding energy to your soul search. When you are calm, your world is calm.

Orthoclase is part of the feldspar family and is a gemstone.

Mother of Pearl

Rainbows of color are visible under a veil of white in this member of the shell family. We all have rainbows in our thoughts. Use this shell to bring some of these rainbows through your own veil of white. This pure white light allows love to manifest in rainbows.

Mother of Pearl is part of the shell or organic family.

Pearls

Work to balance your energy.

Black Pearls - Represent a whole wealth of inner understanding. Decipher top priority on down in your universe. Bring into focus that which is of import today. Knowing which problems to give attention to is very helpful toward daily balance.

Blue/Gray Pearls - Be aware and psychically in tune with verbalization. Bring a balance along with intuition of what must leave you in a verbal way.

Blush Pearls - Create your own comfort and joy while being balanced in femininity.

Brown Pearls - Bring in a balance of grounded, healing energy to femininity.

Green Pearls - Reveal how your longing for things to change externally can't happen until they change internally first. Find emotional balance and change what you can today. Let the rest be distant for the moment.

Peach Pearls - Work on creative energy. Create a world of peace and balance for yourself today. Next, create a whole new world to live in tomorrow.

Pink Pearls - These pearls help provide a nice pillow of inner comfort and acceptance. Comfort your feminine energy with self-love.

Silver/Gray Pearls - Help air out your dark emotional recesses in a healthful way. This brings in transformation to *find* your way.

White Pearls - Bring in a pure balance to feminine energy.

Through extensive research it does not matter if the pearls are fresh water, salt water, Tahitian or South Sea, dyed or natural colors, they all carry the above properties.

Pearls are part of the organic family.

Peridot

Provides mental clarity when looking at past life issues. Know which old issues have value in life today. You can then take proper steps toward the future you desire.

Peridot is also known as Olivine or Chrysolite and is semi-precious.

Peristerite

What clothing do you wear literally or figuratively speaking? Is it truly reflective of who you are? Find the soul's expression and bring it to the surface to be worn with pride!

Peristerite is a gemstone.

Prase

Praise yourself! Praise your ability to speak for yourself! Praise the road you've traveled to become who you are this very minute! Praise the stops along the road in life as well that allow you to catch your breath! (Is a green color)

Prase is also called Edinite, is part of the quartz family, and is semi-precious.

Prehnite

Move from a solid into a liquid with the help of this stone. Remain hardened by life and you are the one that misses out! Find the pillow for the comfort you need, and then go with the flow more easily.

Prehnite is a mineral/gemstone.

Purpurite

This stone can be brown, pink or purple. Regardless of color it helps you feel like a gold rush, pure excitement!

Purpurite is a mineral.

Marcasite/Pyrite

Acts as a generator for protection. Change the inner selective process and eliminate what is negative. Great for those with procrastination as a core issue.

Marcasite is a mineral that does not stand well alone; it needs to be stabilized. Here it is mixed with Pyrite and is a mineral/gemstone.

Pyrite

Also known as fool's gold, it's the proverbial black hole stone in that it takes negativity and sends it to another galaxy. This is the only stone I know of that is self-cleansing. Place a piece near your front door to keep negativity out of your house, or in a room as a type of guard. Pyrite can be useful in eliminating defective red blood cells, though it has not been directed for use in this way as yet.

Pyrite is a mineral/gemstone.

Quartz

Provides Clarity.

Cherry Quartz - Though this is a clear quartz dyed to become this color; it provides clarity for personal creativity. (Is a cloudy peach/pink tone that can be transparent)

Clear Quartz - Shows you clarity and beyond. Knowledge from present and past life is stored within. Take a chance; use it to see where you might have been and where you might go now. (Is transparent to cloudy)

Dendritic Quartz - Provides cool clarity. When thinking long and hard over anything, this stone will give your mind a place to cool down and walk about the thought instead of racing and overworking it. (Is clear with beige, green, white, or even red running through it)

Rose Quartz - Is for self-love. Connects the self with your own heart to know how to care for yourself first. Come from a place of inner strength and then assist others. Do not confuse this with being selfish. There is a huge difference between being selfish and being able to take care of yourself. (Is a light pink tone and can be transparent)

Rutilated Quartz - Far reaching expansion of the mind, assisting to connect the synapses of the brain. Experience the intensity of each thought. Know you make choices all day and night. You shut down on the brain; it does not shut down on you. Let your brain assist in being all that you can be. (Has almost hair-like golden or reddish strands of rutile trapped within the quartz)

Smokey Quartz - Some feel this is a very psychic stone, others feel it is associated with topaz. Actually, it relates to the stresses of the stomach region. Use this stone to find your maleness, then receive clarity as to why you are holding stress in this region. Once done, you can begin to move out of stress.

Each of us contain male and female energy, yin/yang or X & Y chromosomes indicate this. Male energy can express itself as stress in the stomach area of the body. (Is a transparent brown tone. Some call it Smokey Topaz, however, it is not part of the topaz family)

Tourmalinated Quartz - Brings in more clarity while on the search for your life's meaning or purpose. (Is clear quartz with strands of black, green, or pink spikes of tourmaline running through it, usually black)

Quartz is part of the quartz family and is semi-precious.

Realgar

Works on addictions that you know are poisonous to your health.

Realgar is in the arsenic sulfide family and is a mineral. (Wash your hands thoroughly after handling)

Rhodochrosite

Brings forth a connection between your higher spiritual self and the lungs. It teaches you how to breathe and love life. Learn to appreciate even the obstacles in your world today as they lay the groundwork for your life tomorrow. Your thorax muscles which lay between the neck and the abdomen are relaxed with the use of this stone.

Rhodocrosite is semi-precious.

Rhodonite

Is grounded healing light with love. The pink, yellow, green, and brown colors of this stone allow you to cover a lot of territory at once. Love and heal the self with knowledge and instinct. Move on to share this knowledge with others. Come from a place of care and honesty, not self-serving or selfish energy.

Rhodonite is semi-precious.

Ruby

Works from the kundalini or base of the spine on up through the heart chakra showing true love, true hate, or *PASSION*. Ruby energizes you by increasing blood flow while attempting to purify such.

Ruby is part of the corundum family and is precious.

Sapphire
Psychic connections.

Black Sapphire - Protect yourself from spiritual bombardment with this stone. When you are *too* open spiritually, and need protection from unwanted influences, use this stone. Learn how to cut off trickster or draining energy.

Deep Blue Sapphire - Gives the third eye energy center found in the middle of the forehead known as the sixth sense chakra, or intuitive side of your brain permission to open.

Cornflower Sapphire - Works on your psychic connection with the heart. Trust that which in your heart you know to be true.

Green Sapphire - Helps you see wealth blockages and how to push on through these to the other side.

Orange Sapphire - Recreate your destiny by

connecting with intuition and subsequent creative forces. Look at this stone as connecting your inner physical energy with your psychic energy and wow!

Pink Sapphire - Pure love. Love of self, life, the world, and beyond.

Purple Sapphire - Conductor for the third eye chakra. Tune into your third eye to see the guidance you seek for a daily path. Stimulate that energy to grow psychically, emotionally, spiritually.

White Sapphire - Connects with angels. See the good in all, know you are not alone–not ever. Just call and the angels will be there.

Yellow Sapphire - Time to "Stop moping and begin hoping." Trust your instincts to help you move on into the future.

Part of the corundum family, Sapphire is precious.

Scapolite

Don't get stuck in the cracks of life, jump, walk or crawl out of what's holding you back!

Scapolite is semi-precious.

Scheelite

Think of shellac - a great coating that gives way when heated. Show your emotions when moved, and stand firm when necessary for others to see your principles and pride. That's your coating!

Scheelite is a mineral.

Selenite

Is like the shoes you wear, are they old, new, or comfortable? Since your feet are used as directional limbs, it is important to decide if your path in life is old, worn, new, or comfortable, use selenite to decide.

Selenite is part of the gypsum family and is a mineral.

Serpentine

Identify your inner snags.

Black Serpentine - Smile and soothe your inner wrinkles. It doesn't have to be hard work – relax, life unfolds.

Bowenite - Apollo the Greek God comes forth with this stone. When you have worked hard to accept your physical self, use this stone to break down the final door. What walks through the door is the complete you! (Is a light green color)

Stichtite - Rose-red, yellow-green, or purple colors. (See page 98)

Williamsite - Clear to transparent green serpentine. (See page 108)

Serpentine is a mineral/gemstone.

Sinhalite

Sins and halos are contained within us all. Choosing the proper path in life can be hard work or fun. Learn what is proper for you today with the help of this stone.

Sinhalite is semi-precious.

Smithsonite

Regurgitates suppressed emotions. Especially helpful when you have lived in a state of self-denial.

Smithsonite is named for J. Smithson, founder of the Smithsonian Institute, is part of the calcite family, and is a mineral.

Sodalite

Unclutter and calm the mind. This sense of calm will then overlap onto the emotional body, which allows you to live in a more stress-free environment.

Sodalite is semi-precious.

Icelandic Spar

Move without moving. See yourself and life from a distance while unattached emotionally. Decisions of what to do next can be made more easily. This is a great stone to use if you are into astral travel, as one of my spirit guides says, "With spar you can go far."

Icelandic Spar is part of the calcite family and is a mineral.

Spectrolite

Think of the blue, brown, green, orange, and red colors found under the surface of a clear stream of water. Algae and silt help form food substance for fish living in that stream. Use this stone to tap into what provides proper food for you to sustain life. Food for the brain, body, and heart are the subject matter. Be creative in choosing what sustains you today. Perhaps it is not literal food. Grounding rainbows are possible if you make an effort.

Spectrolite and Labradorite (page 70) are geologically the same. Tara-firma separates them along with some of their overall colors. Both are part of the feldspar family and are semi-precious.

Sphene

Your area of activity is expanded with the use of sphene.

Brown Sphene - Activate your home base.

Green Sphene - Activate your heart.

Yellow Sphene - Activate your world.

Sphene is also called Titanite and is semi-precious.

Spinel

Deals with different levels of consciousness.

Black Spinel - Everyone goes into dark emotional places from time to time. Reassessment is a good thing for the soul. Dwell too long and you lose sight of your true path. Black spinel helps guide emotional shut down, or time out periods bringing you back up and out into the daylight again, literally and emotionally.

Blue Spinel - Connects the crown chakra, or energy center found at the top of the head to your third eye chakra, or energy center found in the center of the forehead.

Blue to Purple Spinel - Connects the stream of consciousness you have been working towards and blows the lid off. Bring in the new chosen path with a blast of fresh air.

Green Spinel - Helps reach into your memory banks to find directions you have not yet tried. Perhaps one of those new path concepts is the ticket you have been looking for.

Orange Spinel - Be creative in how you seek spiritual guidance. When ready to receive information trust the form in which the universe manifests it for you. Perhaps a friend or stranger will say something out of context and yet it answers your inner question. Perhaps a magazine article comes into your path that will give insight. Trust the information provided as it usually comes by way of spirit guides who want only the best for you.

Pink Spinel - Is the tactile stone. Realize that what you touch touches you too. Perhaps your hands are on pure Egyptian cotton. Perhaps you are touching ashes. You can and do choose what to touch in this universe.

Red Spinel - Grounding and fulfilling energy are brought forth. Think of how a potato feels in your body. Energetically, this is how red spinel responds to the mind. Feel full, and you relax all over allowing the mind to relax as well.

Yellow Spinel - Breathe from your belly to find new perspectives in daily life.

Spinel is semi-precious.

Stichtite

When easily influenced by others, use this stone to help you stick to your own belief system. Now, blow the socks off preconceived notions of just who you are. (Though it comes in a few colors, rose-red, yellow-green, and purples, this definition overview was given for all tones)

Stichtite is part of the serpentine family and is semi-precious.

Stilbite

Cuts through stored trash. Flake away bit by bit what holds you back from all that is divinely yours with the help of this mineral.

Stilbite is a mineral.

Chinese Writing Stone

Learn how to blossom even in a crowd. Trust the universe has room for you specifically. When you come into full bloom you can propagate or inspire others to do the same. Take small steps to secure the leap, then jump empty handed into the void to write your own story!

Chinese Writing Stone is also called Chrysanthemum Stone, is celestite and shale, and is a mineral.

Sugilite

The great assimilator stone. Work physically and psychically at the same time by cleansing the lymphatic system.
It is a great stone for cancer patients and those with sugar issues. Connect with the crown chakra

found at the top of the head to see what direction to take with food and hopefully with life.

Sugilite is semi-precious.

Sulphur

A necessary mineral for all humans, too much, too little, and you are thrown out of whack. This is one of the best cleansers for your auric field or energy found emanating from and encircling your body. Remember, too much or too little…

Sulphur is a mineral.

Sunstone

Provides rays of light to shine into dark recesses of your soul. Begin to let fresh air into these hidden aspects of yourself with the use of this stone. As with the dawning of a new day, life can be created anew. Be your own creator.

Sunstone is part of the feldspar family and is semi-precious.

Tanzanite

Unites spirituality with the psychic intuitive higher self.

Tanzanite is semi-precious.

Tektite

Helps you with astral travel.

Tektite is part of the meteorite family.

Thomsonite

Wiggle your toes - feel the flexibility they have, give **yourself** permission to experience the same.

Thomsonite is named for Thomas Thompson, and is a mineral/gemstone.

Thulite

Grounds the confused heart. Whether you've gone through an emotional breakup or feel troubled about life's choices, your heart goes into a state of confusion. Use this stone to calm that confusion. With a calm heart, new choices are not only possible, they're plausible.

Thulite is also called Zoisite and is gemstone.

Topaz
Mind expansion.

Blue Topaz - Helps you speak up for yourself while working on bodily water flow. Bring a balance to body fluids and allow yourself to flow verbally as well. (Transparent light blue often confused with Aquamarine)

Green Topaz - Educate yourself. Ask questions and seek advice. Learn more each and every day. (Is a pale green)

Imperial & Precious Topaz - Orange and champagne color tones in topaz assist in past life issues. Clarity is found that can heal old issues, which then help you to move into a new life path.

Pink Topaz - Learn to love the recesses of your mind. Understand how your mind works, then push your *own* buttons and laugh when others attempt to.

White Topaz - Assists in breathing easier after the fog has lifted. You've done the homework. Relax and bask in the newfound knowledge gained from the long journey. For the weary traveler who sees their way clearly now and wants a bit of Rest and Relaxation, much deservedly so. (Is actually a clear stone but referred to as white)

Yellow Topaz - Pucker your lips. Think of sour foods, they're fantastic remedies for the liver where judgment gets stored. Look first to change yourself before looking to change another. Use this stone along with some sour foods to bring a balance to the liver to help change yourself.

Topaz is semi-precious. Even Imperial, and Precious Topaz are semi-precious.

Tourmaline
Great discoveries!

Black Tourmaline - Conducts psychic male energy. Find a balance between male and female brain activity with this stone.

Blue or Indicolite Tourmaline - This third eye chakra stone causes expansion in how you view life and what is important. (The third eye is the energy center found on the forehead, above, and in between the eyes)

Clear Tourmaline - Think of sitting next to a calm stream of clean water and know this form of consciousness can be yours if you really want it.

Green or Chrome Tourmaline - Gives you a direction, life purpose for today, or forever. (Chrome is a specific tone of green)

Pink or Rubellite Tourmaline - Heals holes in the heart chakra allowing for a new lease on life. This can be very traumatic for some people, especially those who have had hard lessons with physical health. Know that whatever comes up with this stone is only a test of lessons learned. Should an old emotional or health issue be brought to the surface, it is simply a gift to now handle the issue in a new way, one that is more healing for you. You can then move on, up, and out of that old issue.

Yellow Tourmaline - Discover your goals and then

know the correct time to act upon change.

Watermelon Tourmaline - Trust and then take a chunk out of life. Enjoy life and use it as a wellspring of opportunity. (This is three or more colors of tourmaline, colorless, pink, or green)

Tourmaline is semi-precious.

Tugtupite

Cleanse your expectations. Are they too far reaching for where you stand today? Are they advanced enough for where you have come from? Only you can decide.

Tugtupite is a gemstone.

Turquoise

Rebirth. It assists in moving forward after much shock to your emotional system. Choose the direction you take now with renewed energy and forthright thought; then all can work out. Trust there is support now. The universe **wants** you to move ahead.

Turquoise is semi-precious.

Ulexite

Magnifies your reality. It has not come into its own as yet, but when it does, Ulexite will carry a message of inner glory. It is also known as TV Rock. You are able to see where you have been emotionally, make peace with such and know it has helped form the you, you are today. Magnify your reality to view how you have developed, and where you might like to go to next. It is especially useful for those in process of **major** change.

Ulexite is a mineral.

Unakite

Is a traveling stone. You may travel emotionally or mentally without physical motion. Truth comes from internal peace. Travel to an internal place – discover your truth, then move *physically* tomorrow.

Unakite is a mineral.

Vanadinite

Think of the sunlight creating diamond sparkles as it shines upon any liquid. You are that liquid, filled with diamond-like thoughts. Tap into your own creative juices to form those diamonds in your daily life.

Vanadinite is a mineral.

Vesuvianite

Don't be alien, learn what your heart desires. Delve down, bring that depth to the surface and live the life you know is yours and yours alone!

Vesuvianite was named for Mount Vesuvius. A mineral whose original name was Idocrase.

Vivianite

Takes you through the door or window you've been facing for some time with a balanced sense of inner grace.

Vivianite is a mineral.

Wavellite

Asks you one question. "Who are you today?"

Wavelite is a mineral.

Williamsite

Fine tune who you have become.

Part of the serpentine family and is mineral.

Fossilized Wood

Trees mark their years of living with rings in their trunks. Use this mineral to make *your* mark on life.

Fossilized Wood is part of the organic family, and is a mineral.

Wulfenite

Sink your teeth into what moves you the most. Passion brings forth understanding!

Wulfenite is a mineral.

Zircon

Connects with stars in our solar system *and* other galaxies.

Blue Zircon - Extra-terrestrial information is at your disposal.

Brown Zircon - Higher intelligence is yours for the asking.

Green Zircon - Heal the planet; it too is a celestial body.

Orange Zircon - Don't bandy about, *move*! With motion comes circulation. Circulation brings energy to the forefront. See how stimulating life can be and how stimulated you can be by life on this planet!

Pink Zircon - Push on through the other side of all blocks with the comfort and support from every particle of God's universe.

Red Zircon - For the right price you can expand your consciousness. Emotionally, spiritually, psychically or mentally, do your work. These are the first steps and first prices to pay. Are you ready?

Violet Zircon - Pokes holes in your consciousness. Don't close the stream of new thought.

White Zircon - The skin you show others should be clear and expressive. Learn the interconnectivity of all things and beings. Incorporate such knowledge into your daily life and routine. (This is a clear stone but referred to as white)

Yellow Zircon - Bring to fruition a childish enthusiasm! Look to the stars!

Zircon is semi-precious.

Thoughts on Metals

Metals also produce energy. Since I am a goldsmith, the metals listed below are what I work with all the time, and as such, what I connect with energetically. This list can help you decide what your next stone purchase might be mounted in for the best personal energetic response. There are other metals such as silver, brass, and copper.

Green Gold - Works with solar energy.

Platinum - Works with solar *and* lunar energy.

Rose Gold - Works with grounding (or the earth's) energy.

White Gold - Works with solar energy.

Yellow Gold - Works with the lunar energy.

Gratitude

My thanks go out to *The Statura Company* for assistance in my learning process of stones, and their family roots. Since I was in college this company has helped me find stones to ignite my curiosity, and my passion for stones of all varieties.

I wish to also thank Pam Potter and William Armitage for their work on editing this book over the course of time. William has also been the driving force to get me to self-publish. He has a great vision if looking for the right fit for *your* literary project!

Please note this book would not have come to fruition if I did not feel such a strong metaphysical connection to my own spirit guides. (Spirits who assist each of us in life) I am sincerely a very lucky person to feel these connections as strongly as I do each day. In my sixties now, I realize how very much a part of my life they all are. Thanks!

Thank you the readers, for sharing an interest in one or more of my passions in this lifetime of jewelry, stones, metaphysics, painting, creating fascinator hats and writing.

I consider myself one of the lucky ones to have found passion at an early age that has sustained me through many years of difficult learning.

Being stubborn, I do not appreciate letting go of old methods of living. Change happens when you least expect it, and it can be the most delightful thing in your life!

Perhaps stones can assist in your quest for betterment, and maybe stones will be magic for you too!

Sincerely

Candace L. Sherman

I would love to hear from you. Feel free to write to me at: cls@clsherman.com

You can also follow my weekly blog at: clsherman.blog

ABOUT THE AUTHOR

Candace L. Sherman is a stone whisperer who lives in Newport, RI. Her life-long passion for stones began in early childhood, as did her gift for making jewelry.

She opened a storefront in 1976 to sell her one-of-a-kind fine jewelry creations. Candace quickly became known for her ability to look at stones and know how they wanted to be mounted.

Through that store, her crystal shop, and her travels with fine art and craft shows, she taught others to work with stone healing energy and color vibrations. Focusing on her ability to channel stone healing properties, she is now sharing her knowledge through books.

Also by Candace L. Sherman

"I have just finished reading
The Crystal Caves by
Candace Sherman. It was a fun
and quick read going through
the caves with the four children
and learning about the
properties of stones and crystals
in a very fun way. The book isn't
preachy but rather very
instrumental to give you sugg-
estions on how to handle our
journey through life with great
lessons and examples."
                    —Amazon Reader

Coming 2020